afternoon tea

afternoon tea is proudly
presented by frankie magazine

afternoon tea and frankie
magazine is proudly published
by morrison media

editor louise bannister
creative director/designer lara burke
photographer cath conroy
chef and food stylist mark core
photographer's assistant mindi cooke
publisher peter morrison

www.morrisonmedia.com.au

www.frankie.com.au

this little book
is dedicated
to all the mums and
grandmas who
taught us how
to cook our
favourite treats.

contributors

LOUISE BANNISTER
EDITOR

Louise was on hand throughout the 'making of' period as recipe chaser and freelance cake appreciator. When she's not drooling over bakery treats, she can be found helming frankie magazine, or dreaming of being fluent in three languages – perhaps so she can say "pass the cake tray" in Spanish, Chinese and Yiddish.

LARA BURKE
ART DIRECTOR AND STYLIST

This delicious collection of treats wouldn't exist without the expertise of Lara Burke. Her creative flair and eye for detail has brought originality to the cookbook genre, not to mention she now has an impressive array of teapots and tablecloths. When she's not designing something spectacular, you'll find her hunting out vintage finds at country op shops.

MARK CORE
CHEF AND FOOD STYLIST

When he's not cooking for the rich and famous in London and Spain, you'll find Mark Core designing car cakes at the last minute and catering for corporates who appreciate a good lunch. His superb baking skills made our jeans tight and our mouths water. Watch this space – Mark hopes to release his own cookbook one day.

CATH CONROY
PHOTOGRAPHER

They say good things come in small packages and pint-sized photographer Cath Conroy is no exception to this rule. Cath's been snap happy since high school and a full time professional photographer for the last five years. A self-confessed part-time daydreamer, Cath's favourite thing to eat was the Lemon Polenta Cake. Her next project involves a great Dane, a girl and inferior baked goods.

MINDI COOKE
PHOTOGRAPHER'S ASSISTANT

When she's not photographing food or interiors, Mindi Cooke is lending her super helpful hands to other photographers. Her most treasured childhood memory is helping her mum choose birthday cakes from old recipe books. And her favourite things to eat on this shoot? A close call between the chocolate éclairs and rocky road.

contents

do you remember a time

when your mother's or grandmother's kitchen
was filled with the delightful smells of baked
goods? Birthday parties would involve homemade
biscuits, marshmallow mouse cakes and vanilla
slice. There were lamington drives and school
fetes, and afternoon tea would mean setting
the brown Laminex table, which extended when
guests were expected.

Homemade childhood treats are something to
be remembered, learnt and passed on, because
the baked impostors in the shops never taste like
Mum's or Grandma's. This book is packed with
40 genuine old-school recipes – recipes that will
bring back the sweet memories of when life was
simple and all that mattered was who would
get to lick the bowl first.

lemon meringue pie

KATE FITZGERALD

To make pastry, preheat oven to 180°C. Combine sifted flours, sugar and butter in a food processor. Blend until mixture resembles breadcrumbs. Add egg and process until mixture comes together in a ball. Cover the dough with cling wrap and refrigerate for 1 hour.

On a well-floured surface, roll the dough until it fits a 22cm pie plate. Lift pastry onto pie plate and gently press into the dish. Trim away any excess pastry. Place a sheet of baking paper on top of the pastry and fill with uncooked rice. Bake for 10 minutes. Remove rice and baking paper and bake for another 10 to 15 minutes, until the pastry is a light golden colour. Allow pastry shell to cool.

To make lemon filling, combine sifted flour, cornflour and sugar in a saucepan. Add the lemon juice. Add 1 cup boiling water and cook until mixture thickens. Add egg yolks, butter and lemon rind, and mix well. Place in cool pastry case.

To make meringue, beat egg whites in a glass mixing bowl until stiff. Gradually add the sugar and beat until thick. Pile on top of filling. Warm in the oven until meringue is lightly brown.

PASTRY

70g self-raising flour

130g plain flour

30g caster sugar

120g cold butter, cut into pieces

1 large egg

. . . .

FILLING

2 tablespoons plain flour

2 tablespoons cornflour

1/2 cup white sugar

1/2 cup lemon juice

2 egg yolks, lightly beaten

1 tablespoon butter

Grated rind of 1 lemon

. . . .

MERINGUE

3 egg whites

4 tablespoons sugar

nelly's apple shortcake
MARK CORE

Preheat oven to 190°C. Grease two 20cm round baking tins.

To make shortcake, in a mixing bowl, cream butter and brown sugar. Beat in egg until combined and fold in sifted flour. Press mixture into baking tins and bake for 15 minutes until golden brown.

Turn out onto wire rack to cool.

To make filling, peel and core apples and cut into eighths. In a saucepan, bring sugar and 1 cup of water to the boil. Reduce and simmer before adding apples. Simmer for 4 to 7 minutes so apples are tender, but not mushy. With a slotted spoon remove apples from liquid and place in bowl to cool.

When both apples and shortbread are cool, place one shortbread-round onto a serving platter and top with apple mixture. Place second shortbread round on top and cover with whipped cream.

SHORTCAKE

90g butter

1/2 cup brown sugar

1 egg

1 cup self-raising flour

· · · · · · · · · · · ·

FILLING

3 Granny Smith apples

1 tablespoon caster sugar

1 cup of water

· · · · · · · · · · · ·

TOPPING

300ml whipped cream

gingerbread
SALLY LAKE

To make gingerbread, preheat oven to 180°C. Grease or line a baking tray with baking paper.

In a large mixing bowl, cream butter and sugar until light and pale. Add golden syrup and egg. Fold in sifted flours, spices and bicarbonate of soda. Turn out onto a lightly floured surface and knead. Wrap dough in plastic and refrigerate for 10 minutes.

On a well-floured surface, roll the dough until it is about 4mm in thickness. Using biscuit cutter in your preferred shape, cut out biscuits. Bake on tray for 10 minutes. Leave to cool on tray for 5 minutes, then transfer to a wire rack.

To make the icing, whisk the egg white until foamy. Add lemon juice and icing sugar and stir until glossy. Tint with your preferred choice of food colouring, and decorate as desired.

GINGERBREAD

140g softened butter

1/2 cup brown sugar

1/4 cup golden syrup

1 egg

2 cups plain flour

1/4 cup self-raising flour

3 teaspoons ground ginger

2 teaspoons ground cinnamon

3/4 teaspoon ground cloves

3/4 teaspoon ground nutmeg

1 teaspoon bicarbonate of soda

ICING

1 egg white

1/2 teaspoon lemon juice

1 cup icing sugar, sifted

Food colouring

banana muffins
MEGAN REEDER

Preheat oven to 230°C. Using melted butter, generously grease a 12-hole muffin pan and set aside.

Sift the flour, salt, baking powder, sugar, cinnamon, nutmeg and mixed spice into a large mixing bowl. Set aside.

In a medium-sized mixing bowl, beat the eggs with a wire whisk or rotary beater until they are pale yellow in colour and fall in a steady ribbon from the whisk. Add the remaining butter, the buttermilk and lemon juice to the eggs and stir well.

Stir the egg mixture into the flour mixture as quickly as possible. Do not over-mix as the ingredients should be just combined. Fold in the mashed banana.

Divide the batter evenly between the holes in the prepared muffin pan. Place the pan in the centre of the oven and bake for 15 to 20 minutes or until a skewer inserted into the centres of the muffins comes out clean.

Remove the muffins from the oven. Cool in the pan for about 4 minutes and then turn them out onto a plate, if you are serving them warm.

Makes 12

MIXTURE

1 tablespoon butter, melted, plus 1/4 cup, extra

2 cups plain flour

1/2 teaspoon salt

2 teaspoons baking powder

1/4 cup sugar

1/2 teaspoon ground cinnamon

1/4 teaspoon grated nutmeg

1/4 teaspoon mixed spice

2 eggs

5/8 cup (155ml) buttermilk (or milk with a squeeze of lemon juice)

1 tablespoon lemon juice

2 medium ripe bananas, mashed

chocolate rum slice
ALLISON SALMON

To make the base, combine finely crushed biscuits, sifted cocoa and melted butter in a mixing bowl. Mix until well combined. Line a 7"x11" lamington tray with aluminium foil. Press mixture onto base of tray only and refrigerate while preparing filling.

To make filling, fill a saucepan 1/4 of the way up with water, and bring to a boil. Cover the saucepan with a tight-fitting bowl. Place marshmallows, milk and chopped chocolate in the bowl. Stir until chocolate and marshmallows are melted. Remove from heat, add rum and cool.

In a separate saucepan, add 3 teaspoons of gelatine to 3 teaspoons of hot water and dissolve. Add to marshmallow mixture.

Fold whipped cream into marshmallow mixture. Pour filling onto prepared biscuit base and refrigerate for 4 hours until set.

Once set, spread extra whipped cream and extra grated chocolate over slice. Cut into squares to serve.

BASE

8oz (240g) plain sweet biscuits

1 tablespoon cocoa powder

4oz (120g) butter, melted

. . . .

FILLING

220g white marshmallows

1/3 cup milk

4oz (120g) dark chocolate, chopped, plus 1oz (30g) extra, grated

1 tablespoon rum

3 teaspoons gelatine

2 cups whipped cream, plus 1 cup, extra, to serve

all together cake
LAUREN BAKER

Preheat oven to 180°C. To make cake, combine all ingredients in a mixing bowl and beat for approximately 6 minutes. Grease a cake tin, pour in mixture and bake for 40 minutes.

While cake is cooling, make the icing. To make icing, mix icing sugar and butter slowly and add hot, not boiling, water while stirring. Add enough water to create a thick consistency, and more icing sugar or butter if needed. Once cake is cooled, apply icing.

Serve with fresh cream and diced strawberries.

CAKE

1/4 cup milk

125g butter

3/4 cup caster sugar

2 eggs

1 tablespoon flour

1/2 teaspoon vanilla essence

1 cup self-raising flour

. . . .

ICING

3 tablespoons icing sugar

60g butter

. . . .

TO SERVE

Fresh cream and diced strawberries

nanna biscuits
HILARY WALKER

Preheat oven to 180°C. In a medium-sized mixing bowl, cream butter and sugar. Add the flour and egg yolk, and mix together to form a dough.

Line a baking tray with baking paper. Roll dough into 16 small balls and place on tray. Press each ball lightly with your thumb to make an indent. Top with a blanched almond. Bake balls for 10 minutes.

Makes 16

MIXTURE

4oz (120g) butter

3oz (90g) caster sugar

6oz (180g) self-raising flour

1 egg yolk

· · · · · · · · · · · · · ·

EXTRAS

16 blanched almonds

small cakes
EMMA FLETCHER

Preheat oven to 170°C. To make the cake batter, in a mixing bowl, beat together sugar, eggs and butter. Add sifted flour and milk alternately. You can add more milk if mixture is too dry.

Grease two 12-hole cupcake pans and divide mixture evenly between holes. Cook for 10 to 20 minutes.

To make icing, beat together icing sugar,2 tablespoons of warm water and 2 tablespoons of butter. Add food colouring of your choice for decoration.

Cool cupcakes completely before icing. For smooth icing, use a knife soaked in boiling hot water to apply.

Makes about 24

CAKES

1 cup sugar

2 eggs

6 tablespoons melted butter

2 cups self-raising flour

1 cup milk

ICING

2 cups of icing sugar

2 tablespoons of warm water

2 tablespoons of butter

Food colouring

raspberry scones
KATE ELLA

Preheat oven to 200°C. Grease a lamington pan or line a baking tray with baking paper.

In a mixing bowl, combine the flour and icing sugar. With the tips of your fingers, rub the butter into the flour mixture until it forms a breadcrumb-like consistency.

Make a well in the flour mixture and pour in the water and milk. Use a knife to cut the water and milk into the flour mix, so it forms a sticky dough. Add the frozen raspberries and cut them into the mix also.

On a well-floured surface, knead the dough until nice and smooth, but be sure not to overdo it. Using your fingers, press the dough out to about 2 to 3cm in thickness.

Dip a scone cutter (or a glass, if you don't have a scone cutter) into some flour, then cut as many scones from the dough as you can. Place the cut-out scones side by side on the baking tray. Knead together the remaining scone scraps and repeat the process until you have little or no dough left.

Brush scone tops with some extra milk then place in the oven. Bake the scones for about 15 minutes until they are nicely browned.

Dust the scones with icing sugar, and serve with double cream and raspberry jam.

Makes 16 to 20

MIXTURE

4 cups (600g) self-raising flour

3 tablespoons icing sugar, plus extra for dusting

60g butter

3/4 cup (180ml) water

1 1/2 cups (375ml) milk, plus extra for brushing

1 1/2 cups frozen raspberries

. . . .

TO SERVE

Double cream and raspberry jam

yo-yo biscuits
MARTINE MERRYLEES

Preheat oven to 160°C. In a mixing bowl, cream butter and sugar. Sift flour and custard powder 3 times, then mix into butter and sugar mixture. Stir in vanilla essence.

Line a baking tray with baking paper. Roll large teaspoons of mixture into balls and place on tray. Press biscuits down lightly with a fork.

Bake on the middle shelf for 15 to 20 minutes. Watch that the underside does not colour too much.

To make filling, cream butter and sifted icing sugar until light and fluffy. Add vanilla essence, then gradually add milk, beating well. This mixture makes enough filling for 30 Yo-Yo Biscuits, which is double the Yo-Yo Biscuit recipe.

BISCUITS

6oz (180g) butter

2oz (60g) icing sugar, sifted

6oz (180g) plain flour

2oz (60g) custard powder

1/2 teaspoon vanilla essence

. . . .

FILLING

2oz (60g) butter

1/2 cup icing sugar

1/2 teaspoon vanilla essence

2 teaspoons milk

betty's caramel tart
BEN SALKELD

Preheat oven to 180°C. Grease a pie dish.

To make pastry, sift flour, cornflour and a pinch of salt into a mixing bowl. Using your fingers, rub the butter into the flour mixture. Add egg and sugar and mix to form a dry dough. Press into pie dish. Bake for 20 minutes.

To make filling, combine sugar and custard powder in a saucepan and, pouring in a little of the milk, mix until you form a smooth dough. Add the rest of milk, egg yolks and butter. Stir over low heat until mixture boils and thickens. Transfer to cooked pastry shell.

Make a meringue topping. Beat egg whites until thick. Gradually add sugar. Spread egg mixture evenly over top of the caramel filling, then brown under grill or stove.

PASTRY

1 1/4 cups self-raising flour

1 tablespoon cornflour

Salt

90g butter

1 egg

1/4 cup sugar

FILLING AND TOPPING

1 cup brown sugar

2 tablespoons custard powder

1 1/2 cups milk

2 eggs, separated

1 dessertspoon butter

1 dessertspoon caster sugar

snowballs
LOUISE MURPHY

To make sponge, preheat oven to 190°C. Grease or line a rectangle baking tray with baking paper.

In a mixing bowl, beat eggs and sugar until fluffy. Fold in flour. Pour mixture into prepared tin. Bake for 20 minutes or until top of cake springs back lightly when pressed. Cool in pan over a wire rack.

To make mock cream, cream butter and sugar. Slowly add milk, 1 tablespoon hot, not boiling, water and vanilla essence. Whip until thick and creamy.

To assemble snowballs, cut sponge in half lengthways and spread the base with strawberry jam. Place top of cake back onto the base. Place in freezer and freeze overnight. While still frozen, use a scone cutter to cut as many circles from the cake as you can. Ice surface of sponge circles with mock cream. Roll snowballs in coconut, then refrigerate until serving.

Makes 12 to 16

SPONGE

6 eggs

200g caster sugar

170g self-raising flour

. . . .

MOCK CREAM

4 tablespoons butter

3 tablespoons caster sugar

2 tablespoons milk

1/2 teaspoon vanilla essence

. . . .

EXTRAS

Strawberry jam [enough to spread over slab]

2 cups desiccated coconut, to roll balls in

apple and sour cream slice
SARAH DODOO

Preheat oven to 200°C. Line a medium-sized baking tin with baking paper.

To make base, combine all ingredients in a mixing bowl, mix well. Transfer mixture to tin and press into the base.

To make topping, mix together apple, sour cream and egg and pour over the base. Sprinkle with nutmeg and bake for 40 minutes. Allow to cool then cut into slices.

BASE

1 vanilla cake packet mix

1 cup desiccated coconut

125g melted unsalted butter

· · · · · · · · · · · ·

TOPPING

410g can pie apples

1 carton sour cream

1 egg

1/2 teaspoon nutmeg

apple and cinnamon muffins
RACHEL CLARE

Preheat oven to 180°C. Generously grease two 6-hole muffin pans. In a large mixing bowl, combine the sifted flours, sugar, cinnamon and apple. Add the milk, eggs, oil and vanilla and stir until just combined. Do not over-mix. Divide mixture evenly between the holes and bake for 30 minutes or until the muffins are golden brown.

TIP You can replace the apples with: 1/2 cup chopped dark chocolate; 1/4 cup chopped dried apricots and 1/4 cup coconut; 1/2 cup raspberries and 1/2 cup chopped white chocolate; 1/2 cup blueberries; or 1/2 cup coconut and 1/4 cup lemon juice.

Makes 12

MIXTURE

3 cups self-raising flour

1 cup plain flour

1 cup sugar

1 teaspoon cinnamon

2 apples, deseeded and chopped

2 cups milk

2 eggs

1 cup vegetable oil

1 teaspoon vanilla essence

best-ever choc chip cookies
PIP LINCOLNE

Preheat oven to 160°C. Using an electric mixer, cream butter with sugars until pale. Beat in eggs and vanilla until combined. Beat in sifted flour until mixed through. Fold through choc chips.

Grease or line a baking tray with baking paper. Roll dough into teaspoon-sized balls and place on tray. Bake for 10 to 12 minutes. If you like them chewy, don't let them brown as they will crisp up as they cool down.

Makes about 48

MIXTURE

125g salted butter

1/2 cup white sugar

1/2 cup brown sugar

2 small eggs

1 to 2 drops vanilla essence

1 3/4 cups self-raising flour

250g choc chips

lemon polenta cake
NADIA MIZNER

Preheat oven to 170°C. Grease a 25cm springform tin. In a mixing bowl, combine the butter, sugar and lemon zest and beat until thick and pale. Keep beating while you add the eggs, one at a time. Stir in the lemon juice, vanilla, almond meal, polenta and baking powder. Mix thoroughly. Knock the bowl against a hard surface occasionally, to make sure there are no air bubbles.

Bake for 1 hour, and then reduce oven temperature to 160°C. Bake for another 40 minutes. Keep an eye on the colour – if it's browning quickly, cover it with foil for the last half hour of baking.

MIXTURE

500g butter, softened

500g caster sugar

Zest and juice of 3 lemons

6 large eggs

2 teaspoons vanilla extract

500g almond meal

300g polenta

2 teaspoons baking powder

lorraine's small éclairs
LOUISE BANNISTER

To make éclairs, preheat oven to 230°C. In a saucepan, combine water, margarine and sugar. Beat gently over heat until melted. Remove from heat and add sifted flour and baking power. Stir rapidly.

Return to heat and cook, stirring all the time until it forms a ball and leaves the side of the pan clean. Remove from heat. Cool slightly and add beaten eggs slowly, stirring.

Grease or line a baking tray with baking paper. Place teaspoons of the mixture on tray. Bake for 20 to 25 minutes. Turn off oven and leave for another 10 minutes.

To make chocolate icing, sift icing sugar and cocoa in a mixing bowl. Add milk, then butter and mix together until the mixture forms a paste.

Fill éclairs with whipped cream and top with chocolate icing.

Makes about 16

ÉCLAIRS
250ml water

1oz (30g) margarine

1 teaspoon sugar

3oz (90g) plain flour

1 teaspoon baking powder

2 whole eggs, plus 1 egg yolk, beaten

. . . .

CHOCOLATE ICING
2 cups icing sugar

2 tablespoons cocoa powder

2 tablespoons milk

2 teaspoons soft butter

. . . .

FILLING
300ml thickened cream, whipped

crunchy pink slice
LARA BURKE

Preheat oven to 140°C. Grease a square slice tin.

In a mixing bowl combine butter, sifted flour, coconut, sugar and vanilla. Pour mixture into tin and bake for 30 minutes until golden.

To make icing, use an electric mixer to cream butter and icing sugar. Beat on high, and add small amounts of milk and food colouring until you reach your preferred consistency and colour. Spread icing on warm slice. Sprinkle generously with coconut and refrigerate until cool.

SLICE

5oz (150g) melted butter

1 cup self-raising flour

1 cup desiccated coconut

1/2 cup sugar

1/2 teaspoon vanilla essence

. . . .

ICING

1 tablespoon butter, softened

1 1/2 cups icing sugar, sifted

1 tablespoon milk

2 drops red food colouring

1 1/2 cups desiccated coconut

macadamia beer cake
BENJAMIN WARD

Preheat oven to 180°C. Grease a springform tin.

In a mixing bowl. cream butter and sugar until light and fluffy. Beat in egg. In a separate bowl, sift the flour and mixed spice. Alternately, fold the sifted flour mixture and beer into the batter mixture until combined.

In a separate mixing bowl, combine dates, nuts and extra flour. Fold the nut mixture into the creamed butter mixture.

Transfer batter to tin. Bake for 50 to 60 minutes, or until a skewer inserted into the centre of the cake comes out clean.

NOTE You can vary the beer you use to achieve different tastes. Try Guinness, Coopers or Hoegaarden.

MIXTURE

125g butter

1 cup brown sugar

1 egg

1 1/2 cups self-raising flour, plus 2 tablespoons, extra (for dates to stop them sticking)

1 teaspoon mixed spice (cinnamon, nutmeg, allspice)

1 cup draught beer

1 cup chopped dates

1/2 cup chopped or roughly crushed macadamia nuts

mummy biscuits
LAUREN BRISBANE

Preheat oven to 180°C. Using an electric beater, cream butter and gradually add brown sugar. Add egg and vanilla and beat well. Sift flour, salt and baking powder into butter mixture and stir until you form a dough.

Line a baking tray with baking paper. Roll portions of the cookie dough into balls, place on tray and squash flat with a fork.

Bake for about 20 minutes or until slightly brown at the edges.

Place on cooling rack for around 5 minutes before dusting with icing sugar.

NOTE The cookie dough can be rolled into a log, wrapped in cling wrap and kept in the fridge or freezer. Just cut off portions and bake as needed.

MIXTURE

6oz (180g) butter

1 cup firmly packed brown sugar

1 egg

1 teaspoon vanilla essence

2 1/4 cups gluten-free plain flour

1/4 teaspoon salt

1/2 teaspoon gluten-free baking powder

simplicity chocolate cake
NADIA SACCARDO

Preheat oven to 180°C. Place butter in a saucepan and melt over heat. Sift flour and cocoa together into a mixing bowl. Add sugar and the lightly beaten eggs, milk, vanilla and melted butter. Stir to combine. Using a wooden spoon or electric mixer, beat hard for three minutes until cake batter changes colour slightly.

Grease and line the bottom of cake tin. Pour mixture into tin. Bake for 30 to 40 minutes or until a skewer inserted into the centre of the cake comes out clean.

MIXTURE

125g butter

1 cup self-raising flour

1/3 cup cocoa powder

1 cup sugar

2 eggs, lightly beaten

1/2 cup milk

1/2 teaspoon vanilla essence

belgian bun
FELICITY WABITSCH

Preheat oven to 180°C. Grease a 20cm cake tin.

To make base, cream butter and sugar in a mixing bowl, then add egg.

In a separate mixing bowl, sift flour, baking powder and a good pinch of salt. Add the butter mixture to the dry ingredients. Mix well.

Transfer half of the batter to cake tin. Spread the lemon cheese over the top of the batter, and then top with the other half of the batter. Bake for about 30 minutes. Allow to cool.

To make the lemon cheese, fill a saucepan 1/4 of the way up with water, and bring to a boil. Cover the saucepan with a tight-fitting bowl. In this bowl melt butter. In a separate bowl, beat egg and add sugar. Stir egg mixture into the butter.

Add rind and juice to the butter mixture. Stir over boiling water until smooth, thick and glossy. Cool before using.

BASE AND TOPPING

115g butter

115g sugar

1 egg

115g plain flour

2 level teaspoons baking powder

Salt

. . . .

LEMON CHEESE

30g butter

1 egg

60g sugar

Finely grated rind and juice of 1 lemon

grandma's fudge cake
ALWYN BARRY

Crush biscuits into fine crumbs. Next, combine butter and sugar in a saucepan and place over low heat, stirring constantly until sugar melts.

Add beaten egg to butter mixture and mix well. Add cocoa and mix well. Add vanilla. Slowly mix in biscuit crumbs until the mixture becomes fairly stiff.

Line a baking tray with baking paper. Transfer mixture into tray. Dust top with coconut and refrigerate. Leave to set for a few hours, then cut into squares and enjoy.

MIXTURE

1 packet Arnott's Marie biscuits

125g butter

125g sugar

1 egg, beaten

1 tablespoon cocoa powder

1/2 teaspoon vanilla essence

Shredded coconut to taste

lemon cakes
CAROLINE STIRLING

Preheat oven to 180°C. In a mixing bowl, cream butter well. Add 1 cup caster sugar and beat again. Add eggs, one at a time, beating well after each addition. Add sifted flour and salt. Add milk, almond meal and lemon rind and fold together.

Grease a 12-hole cupcake pan and divide mixture evenly between holes. Bake in oven for 25 to 30 minutes or until a skewer inserted into the centre of the cakes comes out clean.

Combine lemon juice and extra sugar in a saucepan. Heat until sugar is dissolved. Pour syrup over cupcakes while hot. Cut the slices of glacé orange into small segments (you should get about 8 segments from each slice) and place on top of each cupcake while hot. The lemon syrup will help them stick.

Makes 12

CAKES

125g butter

1 cup caster sugar, plus 1/4 cup extra

2 eggs

1 1/4 cups self-raising flour

1/2 teaspoon salt

1/4 cup milk

1/4 cup almond meal

Grated rind and juice of 1 large lemon

Glacé orange slices

gram's anzac biscuits
BEC THOMSON

Preheat oven to 180°C. Melt butter in saucepan and add syrup. Next, mix bicarbonate of soda in 2 tablespoons boiling water, and add to syrup mixture. In a separate mixing bowl, combine all dry ingredients. Add wet ingredients, and mix well.

Lightly grease or line a baking tray with baking paper. Place teaspoons of mixture onto tray and flatten with a fork. Bake for 15 minutes, then check colour. Biscuits are ready when lightly golden – this will ensure biscuits are doughy rather than tough and crunchy.

Makes 24 small, 12 large

MIXTURE

120g butter

2 tablespoons golden syrup

2 tablespoons of boiling water

1 level teaspoon bicarbonate of soda

1 cup sifted plain flour

1 cup brown sugar

1 cup rolled oats

nanna's peppermint chocolate cake
PRUE VINCENT

To make cake, preheat oven to 180°C. Grease or line a cake tin with baking paper.

Place butter in a saucepan. Melt butter over heat. Next, combine all remaining ingredients in a mixing bowl. Add the melted butter to flour mixture. Beat hard for 3 minutes.

Pour batter into cake tin. Bake for 45 minutes, or until a skewer inserted into the centre of the cake comes out clean. Do not overcook, as it will dry out.

Leave to cool in tin for 10 minutes before turning out onto a wire rack.

To make icing, sift icing sugar and cocoa. Add melted butter and combine until a paste forms. Add peppermint essence to taste. Ice completely cooled cake with a hot knife.

CAKE

3 tablespoons butter

1 cup self-raising flour

1 cup sugar

2 eggs

2 tablespoons cocoa powder

1/2 cup milk

1/2 teaspoon vanilla essence

. . . .

ICING

1 cup icing sugar

1 heaped tablespoon cocoa powder

2 tablespoons melted butter

2 drops peppermint essence

deb's meringues

CLARE MARSHALL

Preheat oven to 110°C. Using a metal bowl and a hand-held electric beater, beat the egg whites until stiff peaks form when you lift beater out of the egg.

Add the sugar in three parts, beating well after each addition. Beat until mixture forms stiff peaks.

Line a baking tray with baking paper. Fill a star-nozzled piping bag with egg mixture and pipe small individual meringues onto tray. Bake for 80 to 85 minutes.

Take meringues from the oven and cool. Serve with whipped cream and fresh berries, or store in an airtight container.

MIXTURE

3 egg whites

180g white sugar

. . . .

TO SERVE

Whipped cream and mixed berries

raspberry and peach crumble
MAI MAI SOMERS

Preheat oven to 180°C. To make filling, combine fruit (including juice from canned berries) in a saucepan. Simmer until peaches are soft.

While fruit is cooking, make crumble. Rub butter, oats or muesli, and flour together in a mixing bowl until ingredients stick together. Add sugar and mix in the remaining ingredients.

Spoon fruit into individual ramekins or one casserole dish. Top with crumble mix, pressing mixture lightly onto the fruit to create a crust.

Bake in oven for 20 minutes until crust is golden brown. Serve with cream, custard or quality vanilla ice cream.

CRUMBLE

1/2 block of butter

1 cup oats or muesli

1/2 cup plain flour

1/2 cup brown sugar

1/4 cup sunflower seeds

1/8 cup sesame seeds

1/4 cup slivered almonds

1/8 cup crushed walnuts

Pinch cinnamon

. . . .

FILLING

500g peaches (deseeded and each cut into 8 pieces)

480g can raspberries (or other berries)

. . . .

TO SERVE

Cream, custard or vanilla ice cream

lemon hazelnut syrup loaf
ALLISON COLPOYS

Preheat oven to 180°C. Grease a loaf tin.

In a mixing bowl, cream butter well, add sugar and beat again. Add eggs one at a time, beating well after each addition. Add sifted flours and salt, and milk, alternately. Add nuts and lemon rind. Pour mixture into tin and bake for 40 to 45 minutes.

In a saucepan, combine lemon juice with extra sugar and stir over low heat until sugar is dissolved. Pour the syrup over the cake while still hot from the oven. Cake can be left to cool in the tin.

MIXTURE

125g butter

1 cup caster sugar, plus 1/4 cup, extra

2 eggs

1 cup self-raising flour

1/2 cup plain flour

1/2 teaspoon salt

1/2 cup milk

1/4 cup chopped hazelnuts

Grated rind and juice of 1 large lemon

honey snaps
NATASHA CANTWELL

Preheat oven to 180°C. In a saucepan, heat honey, sugar and margarine until melted. Remove from heat.

Grease or line a baking tray with baking paper. Sift all dry ingredients into the saucepan and mix well. Drop teaspoons of the mixture onto the cold tray. Bake for 10 minutes.

Makes 12 to 16

MIXTURE

3 tablespoons honey

2 tablespoons sugar

50g margarine

1/2 cup plain flour

1 teaspoon baking powder

1/2 teaspoon salt

1/2 teaspoon ground ginger or cinnamon

carrot cake
VICTORIA HANNAN

Preheat oven to 160°C. Grease a deep 23cm round cake tin by brushing with melted butter or oil. Line the base and sides with baking paper.

To make the cake, sift the flours, spices and bicarbonate of soda into a mixing bowl, then make a well in the centre of dry ingredients.

In a large pouring jug, whisk oil, sugar, eggs and syrup until combined. Gradually stir this mixture into the dry ingredients. Stir until smooth.

Stir carrot and nuts into batter. Spoon the mixture into the prepared tin and smooth the surface. Bake for an hour, or until a skewer inserted into the centre of the cake comes out clean.

Leave the cake to cool in the tin for at least 15 minutes before turning onto a wire rack.

To make icing, combine cream cheese and butter and beat until smooth. Gradually add icing sugar alternately with the vanilla and juice, beating until light and creamy. Spread the icing over cooled cake.

CAKE

1 cup self-raising flour

1 cup plain flour

2 teaspoons ground cinnamon

1 teaspoon ground ginger

1/2 teaspoon ground nutmeg

1 teaspoon bicarbonate of soda

1 cup vegetable oil

1 cup lightly packed soft brown sugar

4 eggs

1/2 cup golden syrup

2 1/2 cups grated carrot

1/2 cup chopped walnuts

ICING

175g cream cheese

60g butter

1 1/2 cups icing sugar

1 teaspoon vanilla extract

1 to 2 teaspoons lemon juice

caramel slice
MELINA JEWELL

Preheat oven to 180°C. Grease a 28cm x 18cm lamington tin or slab tin. Sift flour into a mixing bowl. Mix in sugar and coconut, then stir in melted butter or margarine. Press mixture into tin. Bake for about 15 minutes or until golden brown.

Meanwhile, place remaining butter or margarine in a small saucepan. Melt over low heat. Stir in syrup and the condensed milk. Pour liquid mixture over cooked base, return to the oven and cook for another 8 minutes, or until bubbles form over the top of the caramel. Set aside until cold.

Next, fill a saucepan 1/4 of the way up with water, and bring to a boil. Cover the saucepan with a tight-fitting bowl. Place roughly chopped chocolate and Copha in the bowl and stir until melted and combined. Spread chocolate mixture over caramel topping and chill.

NOTE The best way to cut the slab into pieces is with a large knife that's been dipped in hot water. Make sure that you wipe your knife with paper towel between each cut.

BASE AND FILLING

1 cup plain flour

1/2 cup loosely packed brown sugar

1/2 cup desiccated coconut

125g butter or margarine, melted, plus 60g extra

2 tablespoons golden syrup

395g condensed milk

. . . .

TOPPING

125g cooking chocolate

60g Copha

lemon curd tartlets
MUFFIE SPROAT

Preheat oven to 180°C. Grease two 6-hole patty cake pans.

To make pastry, in a mixing bowl, beat butter until creamy, add sugar and beat until just combined. Add egg gradually, being careful not to over-beat. Work in sifted flours with wooden spoon until you have formed a dough.

On a well-floured surface, knead the dough until nice and smooth. Cover ball of dough in cling wrap and refrigerate for 30 minutes.

Roll out dough very thinly (about 4mm thick) and, using a biscuit cutter or glass, cut out 6cm rounds. Place rounds in prepared pans and bake for 10 minutes. Keep an eye on the pastry, as it can burn very quickly.

To make lemon curd, fill a saucepan 1/4 of the way up with water, and bring to a boil. Cover the saucepan with a tight-fitting bowl. Place all ingredients in the bowl and cook over the boiling water until thick. You can keep lemon curd reserved until needed.

To serve, place a spoon of lemon curd into each tart case. Serve with a little bit of cream.

Makes 12

PASTRY

90g butter

1/4 cup icing sugar

1 egg, beaten

1 cup plain flour

1/4 cup self-raising flour

1/4 cup cornflour

. . . .

LEMON CURD

100g butter

225g caster sugar

2 egg yolks, plus 4 whole eggs (beaten together)

Finely grated rind and juice of 2 lemons

. . . .

TO SERVE

Cream

ruby's coffee cake
GEMMA HANSEN

Preheat oven to 180°C. Grease and flour a 20cm round cake tin.

To make batter, beat eggs until light in colour. Add sugar slowly (one tablespoon at a time) and beat well. Stir in melted butter.

In a separate bowl sift together flour, baking powder and salt. Add 1/3 to the batter mix. Continue adding dry ingredients and milk alternately until all ingredients are combined.

To make filling, combine brown sugar, sifted flour, cinnamon, cloves, melted butter, a pinch of salt and chopped walnuts.

Pour half the batter into the cake tin. Sprinkle half the filling on top. Pour the remaining batter on top followed by the rest of the filling.

Bake for 50 to 60 minutes and serve warm.

BATTER

2 eggs

1 cup sugar

1/4 cup melted butter

1 1/2 cups plain flour

1 1/2 teaspoons baking powder

1/4 teaspoon salt

1/2 cup milk

FILLING

1/2 cup brown sugar

1 teaspoon plain flour

1 teaspoon cinnamon

Large pinch ground cloves

1 dessertspoon melted butter

Salt

1/4 cup chopped walnuts

afghan biscuits
NATASHA LINSKILL

Preheat oven to 180°C. In a mixing bowl, cream butter and sugar until light and fluffy. Sift in flour and cocoa, and mix. Fold in the cornflakes and crushed walnut pieces until just mixed.

Line a baking tray with baking paper. Spoon mounds, as big or small as you like, onto tray. You may need to press each mound together slightly, as the mixture can be dry. Bake for about 15 minutes until just set. Try not to dry them out too much, as it's already a crumbly biscuit.

While the biscuits are cooling, fill a saucepan 1/4 of the way up with water, and bring to a boil. Cover the saucepan with a tight-fitting bowl. Place the chocolate in the bowl and melt over the boiling water. When the biscuits are cooled, ice each biscuit with a dollop of the melted chocolate. Top with a walnut half in the centre.

Makes 12 to 16

MIXTURE

200g softened butter

1/2 cup sugar

1 1/4 cups plain flour

1/4 cup cocoa powder, or more to taste

2 cups cornflakes

1 cup walnuts, crushed

. . . .

ICING

1 block dark or cooking chocolate

6 to 8 walnuts, halved

fruit jelly
AMANDA FOSTER

Divide strawberry pieces evenly between 4 individual jelly moulds.

Make jelly following the packet directions. Pour enough jelly into each mould to just cover the strawberries. Set aside remaining jelly mixture – do not chill. Refrigerate moulds for 5 minutes.

Top moulds with blueberries and a little more jelly mixture. Refrigerate for a further 5 minutes. Then top with blackberries. Fill moulds with remaining jelly mixture and refrigerate for 1 hour or until set.

MIXTURE

4 strawberries, hulled and quartered

1 packet mix strawberry jelly

1/2 cup blueberries

1/2 cup blackberries

chocolate balls
SARA HINGLE

In a saucepan, combine sugar, butter, cocoa, milk and vanilla. Bring to the boil, then immediately remove from heat.

Add rolled oats, toasted muesli and coconut, and mix well. Allow to cool before rolling into little balls. Roll the balls in the extra coconut. Place in refrigerator before serving.

Makes 24

MIXTURE

1 1/2 cups sugar

125g butter

3 tablespoons cocoa powder

1/2 cup milk

1 teaspoon vanilla essence

2 cups rolled oats

1 cup toasted muesli

1 cup desiccated coconut, plus extra for coating

date and nut loaf
ANNA KRIEN

Preheat oven to 180°C. Grease or line a loaf tin with baking paper.

Combine dates and bicarbonate of soda with 3/4 cup boiling water. Leave to cool.

In a mixing bowl, cream butter and sugar until light, white and fluffy. Mix in beaten egg, dates, sifted flour, walnuts and vanilla essence. Pour into prepared tin and bake for 1 hour or until a skewer inserted into the centre of the loaf comes out clean.

Leave cake in tin to cool for 10 minutes before turning out onto a wire rack.

MIXTURE

1 cup chopped dates

1 teaspoon bicarbonate of soda

60g butter

2/3 cup caster sugar

1 egg

1 1/2 cups plain flour

1/2 cup chopped walnuts

2 drops vanilla essence

rocky road
KAITLIN BAKER

Fill a saucepan 1/4 of the way up with water, and bring to a boil. Cover the saucepan with a tight-fitting bowl. Break up both blocks of chocolate and melt in the bowl over the boiling water. Remove from the heat.

Dice Turkish Delight into small cubes. When chocolate is melted add Turkish Delight, marshmallows and cashews. Mix so all ingredients are covered in chocolate.

Line a baking tray with cling wrap. Pour mixture onto tray (it can be a novelty shaped tray) and refrigerate overnight. Once set cut into pieces and serve.

MIXTURE

1 family-sized block Cadbury Dairy Milk chocolate

1 family-sized block Cadbury Dairy Milk Cashew Nut chocolate

100g authentic Turkish Delight (rose and vanilla dusted cubes)

2 packets white and pink marshmallows

100g unsalted cashews, roughly halved

marshmallow tart

ANDREA VANCEA

Preheat oven to 180°C. Grease a tart tray.

To make the tart shell, place all the ingredients into a food processor and pulse until just combined. Roll mixture gently in a ball, cover in cling wrap and refrigerate for 1 hour. Roll pastry onto floured bench or board. Lay over tart dish and press gently to fit. Trim any excess edges. Place a sheet of baking paper on top of the pastry and fill with uncooked rice. Bake for 10 minutes. Remove rice and baking paper and bake for 10 to 15 minutes more, until the pastry is a light golden colour. Allow pastry shell to cool.

To make the filling, place marshmallows in a bowl and add just enough port or sherry to cover them. Soak for about half an hour. In a mixing bowl, combine marshmallows, pineapple, condensed milk and whipped cream.

Transfer filling into tart shell and sprinkle with toasted coconut.

TART SHELL

70g self-raising flour

130g plain flour

30g caster sugar

120g cold butter, cut into pieces

· · · · · · · · · · ·

FILLING

1 packet pink and white marshmallows

150ml port or sherry

450g tin crushed pineapple, drained

200g condensed milk

600ml thickened cream, whipped

1/2 cup toasted shredded coconut

OUR afternoon tea
contributors share
their childhood
cooking memories.

PAGE 12, MARK CORE,
NELLY'S APPLE SHORTCAKE
"Nelly's Apple Shortcake was passed on
to my nan by her best friend, Nelly, when
she was a young lady. My nan then passed
it on to my mother. Mum has been making
Nelly's Apple Shortcake for as long as I
can remember. It reminds me mostly of
birthdays when I was growing up."

PAGE 16, MEGAN REEDER,
BANANA MUFFINS
"Mum and I used to have baking
weekends. My job was to lick the spoon,
although this is actually better suited
to chocolate cakes rather than muffins.
These muffins are best eaten fresh out
of the oven with lots of real butter and
served with coffee. Somehow they
don't taste the same when I make
them. She still bakes them whenever
I visit her in cold Canberra and it
always warms me up."

PAGE 11, KATE FITZGERALD,
LEMON MERINGUE PIE
"My fondest memory of cooking when
I was little is me waiting for Mum to
come home, and then waiting for the pies
to set. My face would end up covered in
lemon and egg white, because my nan
always let me lick the bowl."

PAGE 15, SALLY LAKE,
GINGERBREAD
"I wasn't lucky enough to bake with my
grandmothers, however I did acquire
a cookbook belonging to my maternal
grandma, which was graciously passed
on to me by my own mum. This recipe is
adapted from that book. Baking reminds
me of some very special people who I
have baked with in the past – my Aunty
Alison, my adopted Nanny Baughan, my
ma and my little brother. My favourite
part is still licking the bowl and beaters,
but I will begrudgingly pass this honour
to any small child in the vicinity. And I
never cook without wearing an apron."

PAGE 19, ALLISON SALMON,
CHOCOLATE RUM SLICE
"Having a cuppa is an institution in
my family! We are always eating sweet
treats and drinking sweet, strong tea.
This slice is a big favourite, particularly
when there is a little bit of extra rum
thrown in."

PAGE 20, LAUREN BAKER,
ALL TOGETHER CAKE
"Going to Nan's in the winter and having celery soup and scones is a favourite memory of mine. I still love going there for afternoon tea; enjoying her wonderful company and fantastic cooking is one of the most treasured things I do!"

PAGE 24, EMMA FLETCHER,
SMALL CAKES
"I remember my sister and I were always experimenting with coloured icing. The day we made bright green cakes, there were plenty left over. For some reason it seems only children find bright green cupcakes appealing!"

PAGE 28, MARTINE MERRYLEES,
YO-YO BISCUITS
"When I was little, some of the best family occasions were the ones held at my Aunty Thelma's. She used to put on the biggest, most decadent afternoon teas and it wasn't unusual to be baking for days beforehand. One of the things Mum always made when she baked was Yo-Yos. My job involved pressing each buttery ball with a fork before she whisked them into the oven. They were huge – too big for a little girl to eat. But that never stopped me trying."

PAGE 23, HILARY WALKER,
NANNA BISCUITS
"My nanna often made us her Nanna Biscuits to have on our birthdays. Sometimes she did them with glacé cherries, but I liked the almond ones best. They were the kind of thing she always had in her cupboard, and when we visited we'd hunt for them in the pantry. One was never enough for me. I make them now because Nanna doesn't bake anymore, but they're never as good as hers."

PAGE 27, KATE ELLA,
RASPBERRY SCONES
"Nanna and I have cooked together since I was five. She taught me how to master meringues and how to perfect scones (apart from one salty disaster when she mistook bicarbonate of soda for caster sugar). She gave me a passion for cooking, and I'll always remember her tricks in the kitchen."

PAGE 31, BEN SALKELD,
BETTY'S CARAMEL TART
"To this day I am yet to find a dessert that makes me feel this happy. The smell of caramel and meringue wafting through the kitchen – everything about this dessert is perfect. As a kid, I'd always want to help Mum cook her cakes and desserts so I could lick the bowl and sneak a spoon full of mixture when she wasn't looking. Now, when I visit home, my gorgeous mum always cooks this pie on my last night."

PAGE 32, LOUISE MURPHY,
SNOWBALLS
"It was a tradition in our family to have Snowballs at Christmas time. I remember when dessert was served, all the children would literally run to the table to get the first Snowball!"

PAGE 36, RACHEL CLARE,
APPLE AND CINNAMON MUFFINS
"My grandmother tells me a story of how when my sister came home from school one day, she came into the kitchen to see me (who wasn't old enough to go to school) standing with oven mitts on after just having taken a tray of muffins out of the oven. I said to my sister, 'You can't have any until they cool down!'"

PAGE 40, NADIA MIZNER,
LEMON POLENTA CAKE
"As well as the Lemon Polenta Cake my Mum also used to make cookies. The recipe was given to her by a nurse at the hospital where I was born, and I grew up baking them with her. I like to keep some of the dough ready in the freezer so there is always a fresh batch of cookies 15 minutes away."

PAGE 35, SARAH DODOO,
APPLE AND SOUR CREAM SLICE
"The major part I played in family cooking, was helping with the cleaning. This usually meant licking the bowl and wooden spoon! Apart from that I didn't really cook; I just finished off everything that was cooked!"

PAGE 39, PIP LINCOLNE,
BEST-EVER CHOC CHIP COOKIES
"When I was a little girl, I used to sit in our lounge room after kindergarten and watch Sesame Street. My nan would bring me afternoon tea on a tray. It was a sugary assortment of treats: lamingtons, jelly cakes, coconut tarts and chocolate chip cookies! Baking = Love."

PAGE 43, LOUISE BANNISTER,
LORRAINE'S CHOCOLATE ÉCLAIRS
"I have fond memories of my mum cooking all sorts of yummy treats, especially when it came to our birthdays – I'll never forget the Cinderella cake she once made. To this day, we're always swapping recipes. I love how she just knows what goes together; I hope I have that kind of wisdom one day. These chocolate éclairs are delicious and so easy to make. And who doesn't like pastry with cream?"

PAGE 44, LARA BURKE,
CRUNCHY PINK SLICE

"There was no such thing as 'bought' biscuits in our house when I was growing up. Mum baked all our afternoon tea sweet treats and they were delicious. Her recipe book is full to the brim of hand-me-down recipes. One of our favourite past times was to pretend we were on a cooking show."

PAGE 48, LAUREN BRISBANE,
MUMMY BISCUITS

"The smell of Mummy Biscuits baking always brings back fond childhood memories of me and my sisters helping (or hindering!) Mum in the kitchen. We'd always be jostling each other out of the way hoping to be the one to get to lick the spoon. Now, whenever I bake them myself, I can't help but get nostalgic when the sweet, delicious smell starts wafting from the oven."

PAGE 52, FELICITY WABITSCH,
BELGIAN BUN

"When I was a little girl, I remember this cake always being a special treat, which made it even tastier! We'd always make it when mum was having visitors, and I remember looking forward to when they left so I could finish off the scraps."

PAGE 47, BENJAMIN WARD,
MACADAMIA BEER CAKE

"Oddly enough, beer cake is probably one of my earliest food memories. It was Grandpa Dan's favourite. My grandma used to make it for us when we'd visit them at Christmas. I can still fondly remember sticky summer Port Lincoln days charging around their backyard, ice cream from ear to ear, fistfuls of crumbling warm beer cake in each hand, high as a kite on the sugar rush, whooping it up with my big cousins. Life didn't get much better when you were four."

PAGE 51, NADIA SACCARDO,
SIMPLICITY CHOCOLATE CAKE

"When I was in primary school, cake tins at home were never without a slab of Simplicity Chocolate Cake. Dusted with sugar or smothered in chocolate icing, SCC was a pantry staple. When it came to baking, my mum was the commander-in-chief. As she sifted, poured and stirred, my brothers and I would wait eagerly in the ranks (next to the bench) to be enlisted for the intricate task of bowl licking. Dad would often pitch in, too. When I decided to take the baking reigns, SCC was the first in the mixing bowl. Unfortunately more of the mixture would (and still does) end up in my tummy than the oven. Some things never change."

PAGE 55, ALWYN BARRY,
GRANDMA'S FUDGE CAKE

"Whenever we would visit Grandma, we would always look forward to eating her treats. She always used to say, 'Whoever empties the biscuit tin fills it.' No one would ever want to take the last cake or biscuit out."

PAGE 56, CAROLINE STIRLING,
LEMON CAKES
"I remember the smell of fresh lemon rind and the sound of the electric mixer beating the eggs and sugar. My mum used to let me stir all the ingredients and line the patty cake tins with their paper cases."

PAGE 60, PRUE VINCENT,
NANNA'S PEPPERMINT CHOCOLATE CAKE
"This is my nan's recipe, which Mum and I used to cook together for special occasions. My nanna is still Fay, Queen of the Desserts; she does incredible Jam Roly Polys, but this cake is an all-seasons favourite. Mum's a spectacular cook and I'm forever trying to re-create her talents. Sometimes I'd open my lunch box at school to find a slice of this cake as a treat, alongside a frozen poppa and carrot sticks. Seeing it tucked neatly away always reminded me of how much I loved my mum, and how much she loved me."

PAGE 64, MAI MAI SOMERS,
RASPBERRY AND PEACH CRUMBLE
"Coming from a hippy family – no meat, no sugar, no TV – I can't really remember the moment when my mum decided we would have non-carob dessert at family get-togethers; I just remember most recipes including berries; this one was a favourite. Mum says that the crumble should be served with good quality vanilla ice-cream. Milk products? Wow, she has changed. When my sisters and I moved away, she even gave in and bought a TV."

PAGE 59, BEC THOMSON,
GRAM'S ANZAC BISCUITS
"My grandma is the world's greatest cook. Her luscious scones melt in your mouth although her apple pie is her pièce de résistance. I remember sitting on Gram's kitchen bench, which for some reason we called the 'hoozie'. While I watched her cook, Gram would tell me the story of the naughty Marzipan Man sitting on top of a Christmas cake who 'nibbled the icing till he fell through'."

PAGE 63, CLARE MARSHALL,
DEB'S MERINGUES
"My brother, sister and I loved it when Mum made meringues, which was usually for special occasions. She'd always divide the licking spoils equally; one would get the bowl, one the whisk, and the other the piping bag."

PAGE 67, ALLISON COLPOYS,
LEMON HAZELNUT SYRUP LOAF
"I always remember what a treat it was to be able to lick the bowl or beaters clean after Mum had made a cake. Raw cake mixture is delicious!"

PAGE 68, NATASHA CANTWELL,
HONEY SNAPS

"My mum hardly ever bakes anymore, but when I was a kid she used to make cookies every weekend. She had a recipe box full of hand-written cards passed down from my grandma. Honey Snaps were always my favourite, even when Mum would make a mistake, like leaving out the baking powder. Instead of rising, the cookies would spread out in the oven, becoming crispy hokey-pokey pancakes. Yum!"

PAGE 72, MELINA JEWELL,
CARAMEL SLICE

"My mum and I started making caramel slice for the school fete, and then it became a regular at birthdays and special family occasions. It became so popular that we were asked to bring it along to all kinds of parties. Even to this day we take it to weddings, parties and funerals."

PAGE 76, GEMMA HANSEN,
RUBY'S COFFEE CAKE

"My nan has 12 children, including my mother, so she used to make cake for the family. One of my earliest memories is being in her huge kitchen (which turns out not to be so big now!) when I was about three years old, looking up at this cake and watching all my uncles and aunts drinking coffee and tucking in after they had finished playing tennis. It was my job to sprinkle the dry mixture on top just before it went into the oven. The house was always filled with the smell of cinnamon, cloves and the noise of us grandkids. I remember it very fondly."

PAGE 71, VICTORIA HANNAN,
CARROT CAKE

"My mum used to cook this cake on cold winter weekends, as sheets of rain lashed down on the Adelaide Hills. I have the fondest memories of the smell of cinnamon, ginger and golden syrup, of our kitchen decorated in browns favoured by the '70s, and of Mum in her bright blue pinafore letting me lick the bowl."

PAGE 75, MUFFIE SPROAT,
LEMON CURD TARTLETS

"I can picture Mum and I at our kitchen table, her rolling out the pastry dough for the tart cases, me cutting the rounds and putting them in the patty cake tins, and her putting them in the oven. Both of us in aprons, hers fitting and mine (which was hers) coming down to my ankles. She would be content if they turned out golden brown, but if we left them for a minute longer they burned quickly. This only happened very occasionally but she would be furious! Mum has two levels of burning – level one would go to the chooks, level two (not too bad) would go to Dad!"

PAGE 79, NATASHA LINSKILL,
AFGHAN BISCUITS

"Baking with Nan was always an afternoon-long ritual. It was never just chucking ingredients in a bowl. Every time we'd bake, we'd use the exact same bowls, the exact same transparent green Tupperware strainer, the exact same faded brown plastic spatula that was melted at the tips so it curled up. After our concoctions had baked and cooled Nan would lay her table with one of her own hand crocheted tablecloths, a pot of tea, and some of her amazing teacup and saucer sets. Then the three of us would sit, drink, talk and enjoy the fruits of our labour together for afternoon tea."

PAGE 80, AMANDA FOSTER,
FRUIT JELLY
"The tooth fairy took my sweet tooth many years ago, but fixing up this little treat with my mum brings back many sweet memories."

PAGE 84, ANNA KRIEN,
DATE AND NUT LOAF
"My mum used to have this loaf waiting for us when we got home from school. When we were older, we'd let ourselves in with a key hidden inside a fake rock in the front yard. We grew up in St Kilda and there was an asylum nearby. Sometimes when we came home from school, a man from the asylum would be sitting on the front porch with his suitcase, trying to convince us that he had bought our house from Mum and that we didn't live there anymore. But we always got past him and to the yummy afternoon tea inside!"

PAGE 88, ANDREA VANCEA,
MARSHMALLOW TART
"Growing up, we usually had a special tart made for us on our birthday. My cousins would usually choose apricot or apple tarts but I always wanted a marshmallow tart. It always looked fantastic and tasted even better." •

PAGE 83, SARA HINGLE,
.CHOCOLATE BALLS
"This was my favourite recipe to help Mum make at home in Perth. It brings back vivid memories of being perched upon the lime-green countertop while we waited for the mixture to cool before rolling, which always seemed like an eternity. It was always worth the wait – not only could we get our little mitts extremely sticky rolling the mixture into balls, but it tasted like nothing else. And then there was the next gruelling wait – allowing the balls to cool in the fridge. "Oh well," Mum would say. "You can always help clean up!" That got us out of the kitchen, quick smart."

PAGE 87, KAITLIN BAKER,
ROCKY ROAD
"This treat always reminds me of summer and fun with my family. It's always made for special occasions and is a favourite at Christmas. I still help mum make it every year."

WE'D JUST LIKE TO SAY THANKS. Thanks to Mark who cooked till he could cook no more, Cath for her perfection, Mindi for her helping hands, Peter, Di and Morrison Media for backing us from the beginning, Rick and Ed for their patience and support and last but definitely not least to all our fantastic contributors and their loving mothers and grandmothers who shared their treasured cooking memories. This book wouldn't exist without you. Love Lou and Lara x